A PASSION FOR

cactus

— by —

Jack Kramer

A Welcome Book

Andrews and McMeel
Kansas City

It can seem powerful and fearless, with curved arms stretching out toward a desert sky. It can be a fierce survivor, drawing nourishment from the barren land with a protective coat of spikes for armor. It can be a laid-back housemate, with modest needs for some sunlight and the occasional sip of water. It can be beautiful and mysterious, its flowers blooming brightly, perhaps even during the night. With its sculptural forms, wild spikes, and intensely colored flowers, the cactus demands our attention and captures our imagination.

Fleshy Leaves
[*also called pads*]

Spines

Cactus Flower
[*some varieties bear fruit*]

Water Stored Here
[*body of the plant*]

— • —

basics

The cactus family, Cactaceae, embraces numerous species of succulent, or water-storing plants, most of which dwell in arid climates. Cacti are characterized by flattened bodies, fleshy leaves, spines that can be sharp as needles or fine as silk hairs and, often, large colorful flowers.

While they are mainly desert plants, not all cacti are native to desert areas; some, such as the *Rhipsalis* species, are from rain forests. The cactus family is found in territory that ranges from Canada to Mexico, Central America, the West Indies, and certain cool regions of Chile and Patagonia.

Cacti evolved step by step from primitive jungle plants to highly specialized desert dwellers. The climbing vine called *Pereskia,* native to the West Indies, is thought to be the "mother" of all cacti, the Eocene ancestor from which the modern cactus has developed. The cactus has a rich and varied heritage, spanning from the Eocene age to the present day. It was first used for food by Native Americans and later for sisal, a fiber that can be made into rugs and other woven products. Cacti have been used in a variety of cultures as a source of food, and for medicinal purposes.

Until the discovery of America, cacti were virtually unknown in Europe. Linnaeus, the father of plant classification, first listed cacti in his *Species Planatarum*, in 1753, naming the genus after the Greek *cactos*, which means "thistle." After American cacti were discovered and classified, they were brought back to Europe, where the plants were grown primarily in monasteries. Eventually, cacti became quite fashionable and were planted in botanical gardens throughout Europe.

In addition to symbolizing the gift of the water needed to harvest crops, the cactus has been used to signify the founding of a city. The *Codex Mendoza* was created in 1541–42, a generation after the Spanish conquest. This illustrated book depicts the history of Mexico from 1325 until its demise in 1522. On the folio, *right,* an eagle sits atop a cactus as a symbol to the Aztec empire that the people had reached the promised land of Mexico.

tenochtitlan

42'

39'

36'

33'

30'

27'

24'

21'

18'

15'

12'

9'

6'

3'

carnegiea gigantea   *'51 cadillac sedan*

The giant saguaro cactus (*Carnegiea gigantea* or *Cereus giganteus*) is also called the Sage of the Desert. It towers 50 feet into the air on average, and is the longest living of the American cacti, living for as long as 250 years. The saguaro is one of the best-known cacti, with its familiar candelabra-like branches reaching up like arms toward the desert sky, and giving it an almost human quality.

Found primarily in Arizona, southeastern California, and Sonora, Mexico, this giant cactus can hold literally gallons of water, so it is able to rough it in the desert with no problems. It bears edible crimson fruits and provides a home for a variety of birds, who nest in the tall columns, apparently without fear of their spiny housing.

According to the *Guinness Book of Records*, the tallest living cactus at this time is a saguaro measuring 57 feet 11³/4 inches, located in the Maricopa Mountains

the only known instance of
DEATH BY CACTUS

IN 1984, A MAN IN PHOENIX, ARIZONA, SHOT A GIANT CACTUS TWICE WITH HIS RIFLE, WHEREUPON A TWENTY-THREE FOOT SECTION DROPPED OFF AND CRUSHED HIM

!

Chamaecereus Silvestri, also known as the

peanut cactus

— ✿ —

near Gila Bend, Arizona, discovered on January 17, 1988. The tallest cactus ever recorded was an armless cactus 78 feet in height in Cave Creek, Arizona. Unfortunately, it blew down in a July 1986 windstorm, at approximately 150 years of age. While there is no record of the smallest cactus, living or otherwise, several tiny dwarf varieties do exist, such as the *Chamaecereus Silvestri*, also known as the peanut cactus.

Sunset at
Saguaro National
Monument in
Arizona.

A page
from the
A. Blanc & Co.
cactus catalog,
dated late
nineteenth
century.

Outside of botanists and others interested in plants, cacti were not well known in Europe until the middle of the nineteenth century, when all of England became engulfed in a flower mania. Suddenly, everyone wanted to seek out the strangest and most exotic plants in existence. The leafless, prickly, and weirdly formed cactus fit the bill of **strange** and **exotic** very nicely. At first, cacti could not compete with the beautiful and much sought after orchids. Still, small collections of the plants prospered in many a lord's conservatory and eventually the **bizarre** and compelling characteristics of the cactus drew a loyal following who understood that **beauty** is not always an obvious thing. The most popular species were night bloomers such as the cereus and epiphyllums, a phenomenon previously unheard of in England.

jumping cactus

The cholla cactus, with its armor of daggerlike spines, is a member of the *Opuntia* species. It has been referred to as the **cursed** cholla because it is so **dangerous** to animals, and as the **jumping cactus** since its thorns seem to jump out and prick whatever comes close to it. In the Southwest, medicine men have traditionally used branches of **cholla** in prayer ceremonies to help rid their patients of illness, believing that the sickness will get caught up in the sharp thorns.

left:

section of

red cholla

— • —

opposite:

teddy-bear

cholla

ROLL OUT THE BARREL CACTUS

Although a field of them can resemble a Martian moonscape, barrel cactus is a common species in the wild. Also known as *Echinocactus Grusonii*, these plants are huge and barrel-shaped and look somewhat like giant pincushions. Indigenous peoples of both North and South America used these and other types of globular cactus as altars in religious ceremonies, sometimes impaling effigies upon the spines. A less spiky fact about the barrel cactus is that its bright yellow fruits and flowers grow in a perfect circular pattern at the top of the plant.

An illustration from the A. Blanc & Co. catalog

There is more to the cactus than simple spines and padlike leaves. Cacti can be **whimsical**, bizarre, and incredibly **varied** in structure, from spiral to candelabra, erect, **globular**, and even shaped like stars. Some have growths that resemble organ pipes while others look like giant pillars. From the **woolly** borzicacti to the gnarled Lophophora, these cacti run the gamut of weird and **unusual** forms.

plant shape

clockwise from top left

ridged globe
ferocactus melocatiformis

**globe
(pin cushion)**
mammillaria johnstonii

**columnar
(single or multiple)**
*lemaireocereus
marginatus*

star
astrophytum capricorne

star
leuchtenbergia principis

cascading
zygocactus truncatus

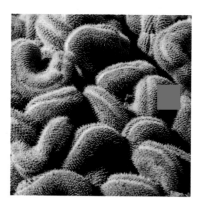

clockwise from top left: **the totem pole cactus, the snake cactus, a section of the boxing glove cactus, the borzicactus celsianus.**

opposite: **these star cacti grow in a spiraling pattern.**

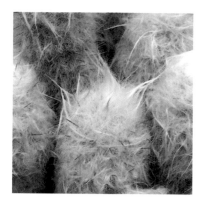

Cacti forms range from the expected to the surreal. *far left:* **A desert vista, resplendent with saguaros.** *near left:* **Two drawings from the** *Curtis Botanical Magazine,* **dated early nineteenth century. These flowered cacti were featured in the periodical as exotics.**

— • —

flowers

A lush bolt of color against dry hostile terrain, the cactus flower seems at first to be an anomaly. Yet this prickly desert plant yields large and vibrant flowers of startling beauty.

Cactus flowers are found in a variety of shapes and brilliant colors, which run the spectrum of yellow, red, pink, orange, purple, and white. These blossoms are often so large that they almost overtake the plant itself. Examples include the one-inch rebutias, notocacti, and parodias, which bear four- to five-inch flowers, and the epiphyllums, which bear flowers up to seven inches across.

notocactus herteri

ferocactus wislizenii

gymnocalycium quehelianum

rhipsalidopsis chertneri

In some species, commonly known as nocturnal or "night bloomers," the flowers open at night and close during the day. One example of this phenomenon is the *night-blooming cereus* also known as Selenicereus grandiflorus.

The
orchid cactus
often grows
plentifully in
jungle areas

— • —

The
lobivia
famatiensis
features funnel-
shaped flowers

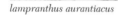

lampranthus aurantiacus

agave victoria reginae

agave horrida

adenium obesum

succulents

dudleya brittoni

While all cacti are succulents, not all succulents are cacti. Succulents do share the smart survival tactic of storing water in their fleshy leaves to survive in arid environments, but they can be found in many other plant families, including the amaryllis and lily. The succulents come in many forms, from hedgehogs (Euphorbiaceae) to pointed dagger-like leaves (yuccas) to pebble-like stones (lithopses). Famous succulents-about-town include the poinsettia plant and the *Ananus bracteatus,* which bears the pineapple, and the agaves, often called century plants, which are believed by some to bloom only once every one hundred years.

far left:
hechtia
gallesbrighti

— • —

near left:
agave shawii

THE HOLLYWOOD CACTUS

top: **A surreal desert landscape helps pay homage to the Western in the**

comedy *The Three Amigos,* which starred Martin Short, Steve Martin and

Chevy Chase. *opposite:* **Jean Harlow poses against a forest of cacti**

in a production still for the 1933 MGM film *Bombshell.*

From across the vast desert terrain, the lone **cowboy** rides his trusty horse into town. He saves the day, he gets the girl, and there in the background is the **cactus**. Serving as a backdrop for such greats as John Wayne and Gene Autry, cacti such as the classic **saguaro** define our romantic notions of the **American West**.

Although it has a reputation as a hardy desert loner, the cactus is actually part of our vast ecological web. **Birds** such as the Gila woodpecker have been known to nest in its spines, and ground squirrels **eat** the **red fruits** of the saguaro. Then you have the lesser long-nosed bat. Like some cactus flowers, these **bats** are creatures of the night, and thus the two make a perfect match. This feisty creature helps **pollinate** the saguaro cactus by transferring pollen from **flower** to flower as it flies and feeds. This is similar to the pollination of flowers by bees, only with a great deal more style.

far left: **The** *lesser long-nosed* **plunges in.** *near left:* **The beak of a** *white-wing dove* **carries pollen from plant to plant while an antelope ground squirrel feeds on saguaro fruit.**

Cooked roots
of Cereus species
can be made into
a poultice to
treat swelling.
This painting by
Door A.J. Van Laren
depicts a
cereus candicans.

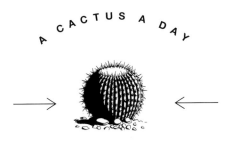

A CACTUS A DAY

keeps the doctor away

The cactus has been recognized as a potential curative in many southwestern Native American cultures. Cacti are believed to **cure** or aid everything from **earaches** to **broken bones**. These **medications** can take several different forms. For example, the cut stems of many cacti serve as a topical treatment for burns, and extracts from stems are used as a possible cure for **indigestion** or stomach problems. Among the cacti most often used for their medicinal properties are the cholla, barrel cactus, organ pipe, and the *Cereus* and *Opuntia* species. The believed uses are numerous. Fleshy tuberous roots of some cacti are used in preparations as a **remedy** against dysentery, while a plaster made from crushed pads can be used to heal broken bones.

far left:

The *golden barrel cactus.* Some varieties of barrel cacti are believed to have medicinal properties

— • —

near left:

The Ferocactus, commonly known as *fishhook cactus.* Juice from cooked stems of the Ferocactus can be used to cure earaches.

"BEAR SHOOK HIMSELF, AND OUT OF HIS FUR DROPPED JUNIPER BERRIES. HE SHOOK HIMSELF AGAIN AND OUT DROPPED A CACTUS THAT WAS GOOD TO EAT. THEN HE SHOOK OUT ACORNS, THEN ANOTHER KIND OF CACTUS...THEN SAGUARO FRUIT."

—

from "Turkey Makes The Corn and Coyote Plants It," American Indian Myths and Legends

B

THE EDIBLE CACTUS

A

While at first we don't think of cactus as something good to eat, many species can be prepared in a variety of delicious ways. One such edible cactus is the prickly pear. Both the pear fruit and the pads are used as food among many groups of southwestern American Indians. But humans aren't the only ones who can munch on the prickly pear. Because they retain water so well, the pads are given to thirsty livestock when there is a scarcity of rain. The prickly pear also creates a formidable fence around cattle ranges. And if all this weren't enough, the plant joints yield a juice that helps heal fractures. The prickly pear fruit is sweet and tangy and is at peak flavor between September and February.

The
hedgehog cactus
(Echinocereus
Engelmannii)
bears fruit that can
be eaten like a
strawberry or
cooked into jam.
A large plant can
yield up to
2 quarts of these
"strawberries."

The pads of the **prickly pear cactus** are referred to as nopales and sold in specialty stores fresh or canned. If bought fresh, the spines should be removed from the pads with a potato peeler or the point of a sharp knife. Also, gloves should be worn.

After cutting nopales into strips or cubes, drop in boiling water, cook until tender, then drain and try them in one of the following recipe ideas. **1** Slice strips and cook with scrambled eggs or fold into an omelette. **2** Slice strips and cook with onions and eggs for filling tacos. **3** Mix strips in salads with avocado and lettuce. **4** Dip strips into batter of one half water and one half beaten eggs, then deep fry until crisp. This makes an excellent appetizer.

For a delicious side dish, try

NOPALES WITH BLACK AND WHITE BEANS

ingredients

6 medium nopales (cactus leaves)

$1/4$ pound butter

$1/4$ pound dried black beans, soaked overnight in water

$1/4$ pound dried navy beans, soaked overnight in water

4 ounces salt pork

2 medium onions

method

To prepare the nopales: Blanch the nopales in a pot of lightly salted boiling water for 4 minutes. Drain and reserve. When ready to serve, melt the butter in a skillet and sauté the leaves briefly on each side. Remove and cut diagonally into $1/2$–inch strips. To prepare the beans: Drain the beans and discard the water. Place the beans in a large saucepan and add water to cover. Add the salt pork and onions. Bring to a boil, reduce the heat to a simmer, and cook until the beans are tender, about 30 minutes. Discard the onions. To serve, spoon the beans over the nopales. Note: The beans can be reheated easily and the flavors are enhanced on the second day. Serves 6

THE TOHONO O'ODHAM

saguaro festival

Each year in the late July heat of Arizona and New Mexico, the Tohono O'odham (or Papago) Native Americans celebrate the Saguaro Festival, which utilizes the well-known cactus in an unusual way: as the main ingredient in a ceremonial wine.

This ceremony, also called the Vitigita, has several functions. It is a harvest feast celebrating the cactus fruit, a rainmaking rite, a blessing for

———————— • ————————

opposite top: **the fruit in its flowerlike pod.** *opposite bottom:* **pouring the syrup.**

opposite right: **picking the cactus fruit.**

the summer crops, and a reaffirmation of community ties. Over the course of several days, dances, songs, and pantomimes are performed, and a "sit and drink" ceremony is conducted on the third day, when the wine is ready to be enjoyed.

The women of the community gather the fruit of the saguaro to be fermented into wine. After it is gathered, saguaro fruit is first cooked, then the juice is boiled into a syrup. This syrup is poured into jars and left to ferment. The wine is kept in a ceremonial rainhouse during this process, which is regulated by the village headmen. It is then served to everyone at the sit and drink ceremony, which symbolizes the rain saturating the earth.

Other cultures view the cactus as emblematic of rainmaking as well. The Diaguita Indians of Chile, who are native to one of the world's driest deserts, the Atacama, invented rainsticks made from cactus to help bring the rain. Quisco cacti, which grow plentifully in the hills, are dried naturally, gathered up, and cut into sticks. The thorns are pounded down until the surface is smooth. Lava pebbles are then placed inside and the tube ends are sealed. When the cactus sticks are turned over, the sound of rain is created by the pebbles, which pour over and around the interior thorns with a gentle woosh.

Tohono O'odham artist Leonard Chana celebrates his childhood memories of the Saguaro Festival in his painting *Carrying Water for Mom and Aunt Molly.*

Various succulents and containers decorate the pool area of this home.

Ficus Indica Fystletten
licet amet lobe erata lu.

In the outdoor setting, the shapes and forms of cacti and other succulents seem more like sculpture than mere ground cover, and have long been popular for landscaping use in the gardens of California, Arizona, New Mexico, and Texas.

To create a well-balanced picture in the garden, consider the size of plants. Large plants are best as both the background and to frame the picture. Torch cactus, fishhooks, and yuccas are perfect plants for this

purpose. Next will be the medium-sized plants, best used around groups of rocks. Finally, plant small cacti and succulents between the rocks. The combination of rocks and plants of varying heights provides a harmonious desert scene.

The garden for cacti and succulents should be in a sunny location. As these plants need perfect drainage when planted outdoors, try to slope or raise the planting bed. Use a light and gritty soil and place a thin layer of crushed gravel or marble chips over the soil after planting, around the roots of the plants, for frost protection.

Outdoor cacti and succulents will need lots of water in the summer, as much as every week if there is no rain, as in northern California. In the spring and fall, the plants need less water. Remember: wet soil and soft growth can kill plants if a freeze hits. Some species are more susceptible to cold than others, so buy your cacti and succulents from local dealers so you will be sure the plants will survive in your area.

— • —

opposite top: **a front entrance flanked by *opuntias*.**

opposite bottom: **trichocereus used as a sculptural accent in an Arizona garden.**

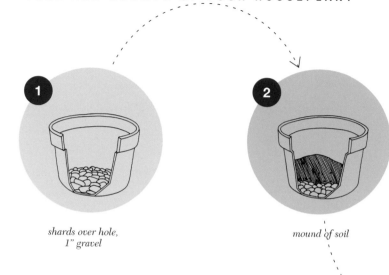

shards over hole,
1" gravel

mound of soil

Cacti are famous for being low-maintenance houseplants. As water is stored in the leaves for up to a month, they can be watered and cared for more sparingly than many other plant families. However, this does not mean they can thrive without any care at all. Here are a few tips to keep your cacti growing strong. **Soil** Contrary to what many people think, cacti do not grow in sand. They need a good nutritious soil mix that is kept well-drained. You can use packaged soil sold for houseplants to which you

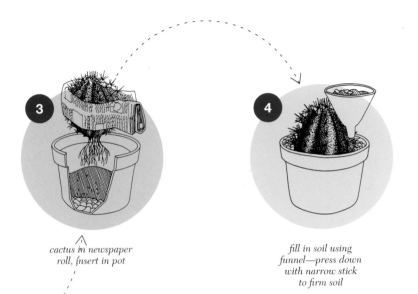

cactus in newspaper roll, insert in pot

fill in soil using funnel—press down with narrow stick to firm soil

have added some charcoal, which can be purchased at most plant nurseries. A handful of sand can be added to the soil to speed drainage and enhance aeration. You can also use soil especially formulated for cacti.

Watering & Feeding As cacti can store water for long periods of time, more care should be taken not to overwater your plants. On average, you can water a medium-sized plant about twice a month or when soil is completely dry. When in doubt, do not water. Apply a standard

20-20-20 houseplant fertilizer twice a month in the spring and summer, once a month in the fall and winter. **Light** Cacti are best grown in direct sunlight. Turn your potted plant every so often so that all parts of the plant receive an equal share of light. Do not turn plants that are ready to bloom, as a sudden change in light can cause buds to drop off. **Potting** The plant and soil mix should be dry prior to potting as excessive moisture can cause cacti to rot. Pot the cactus as you would an ordinary houseplant, but allow to sit for a day or so before watering and then water sparingly for the first few weeks. The spines of cacti are not a problem if you use garden gloves or a folded newspaper when handling plants. See the diagram on the previous page for help in potting spiny cacti.

— • —

plant problems At right is a list of the most common problems associated with less-than-adequate care of succulents or cacti. Unless you detect insects on your plants that could be responsible for poor growth, you should first see if the signs of your plant's ill health are listed in the chart.

SYMPTOM	PROBABLE CAUSE	REMEDY
Failure to make new growth.	*Too much water, or soil is compacted, roots may be decayed.*	*Repot in a fresh soil mixture, adjust watering practices.*
Stems or leaves are yellow.	*Plant is too dry and receives too much heat.*	*Provide better ventilation and more moisture in the air.*
Pale color.	*Root injury.*	*Trim away dead roots or damaged growth.*
Elongated growth.	*Not enough light.*	*Move plant to location with more light.*
Failure to bloom, or very few flowers produced.	*Plant has received too much nitrogen.*	*Use fertilizer low in nitrogen but high in phosphorous.*
Flower buds drop.	*Temperature is too low or fluctuates too much; plant is in draft.*	*Move plant to a draft-free location.*
Soft or mushy growth.	*Too much moisture, temperature too low.*	*Reduce moisture, cut away soft parts and dust cuts with Captan.*
Corky skin on stems.	*A natural development on some cacti as they age.*	
Plant has a glassy, translucent look beginning in fall or winter.	*Frost damage.*	*No cure for damage done; keep plant dry; be sure it is not subjected to such low temperatures again.*

The snakelike
selenicereus
leaps out from
amongst a varie
of cacti.

*For information write:
Andrews and McMeel
A Universal Press Syndicate Company
4900 Main Street
Kansas City, Missouri 64112*

*A Welcome Book
Welcome Enterprises, Inc.
575 Broadway
New York, New York 10012*

Editor: Jennifer Johnson

*Design by Kathleen Phelps,
Platinum Design Inc., NYC*

*Library of Congress Catalog Card
Number: 95-77551*

ISBN: 0-8362-0800-5

*Printed in China by Toppan Printing
10   9   8   7   6   5   4   3   2   1*

Acknowledgments

I would like to thank the following for their advice, information, assistance and wisdom: Janet Cole and Desert Botanical Gardens, Phoenix, Arizona; Mitchell Botanical Gardens, Milwaukee, Wisconsin; Anthony Garcia; Mildred Ford; Windrush Galleries of Sedona, Arizona; Gina Douglas of the Linnean Society of London; M. Dalziel of the Bodelian Library; Marvin Grotell and the Cactus and Succulent Society of America; Casalinea of New York City; The Nature Company and Rodney Todd White.

Special thanks to Lena Tabori and of course to all the artists and photographers whose contributions are on these pages.

And most of all, my thanks to the plants. — Jack Kramer

Art Credits

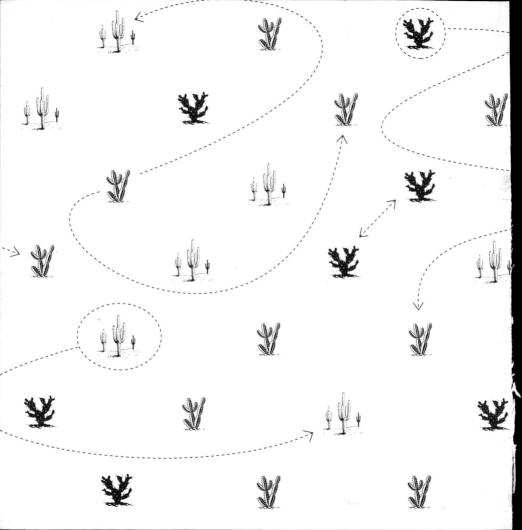